Bitch

A Vulgar Language Adult Coloring Book
For Release Anger

By

S.B. Nozaz

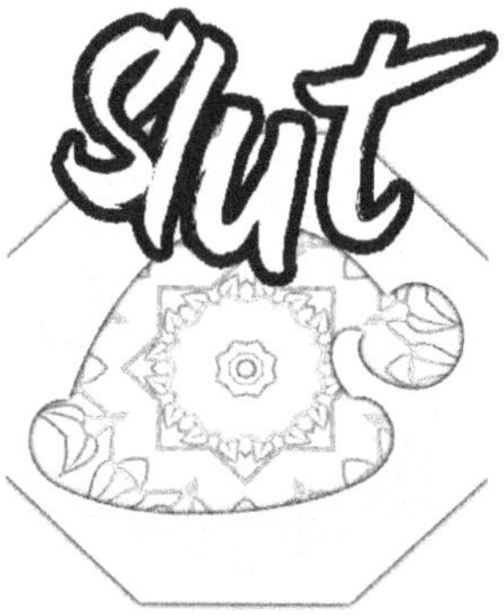

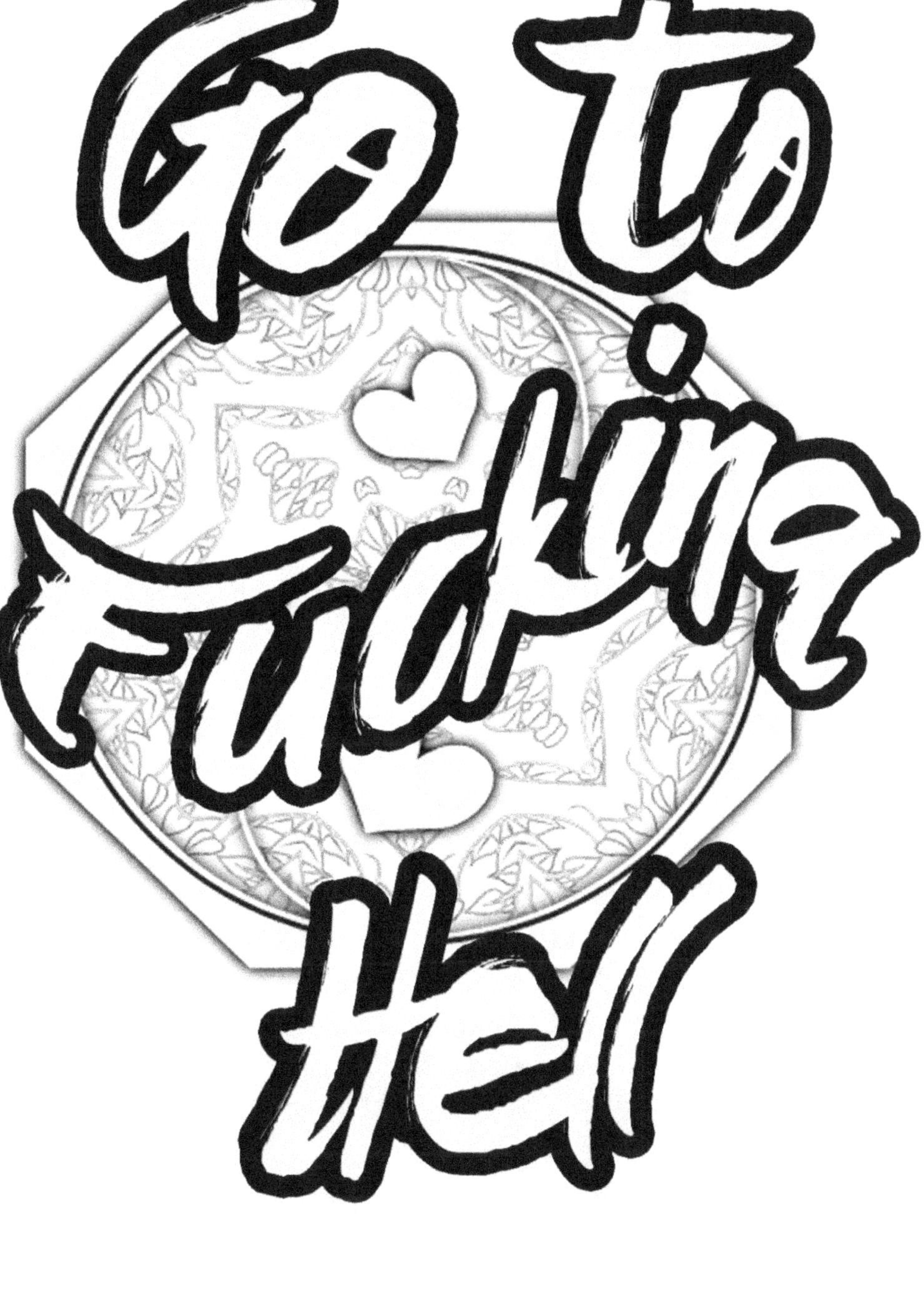
Go to
Fucking
Hell

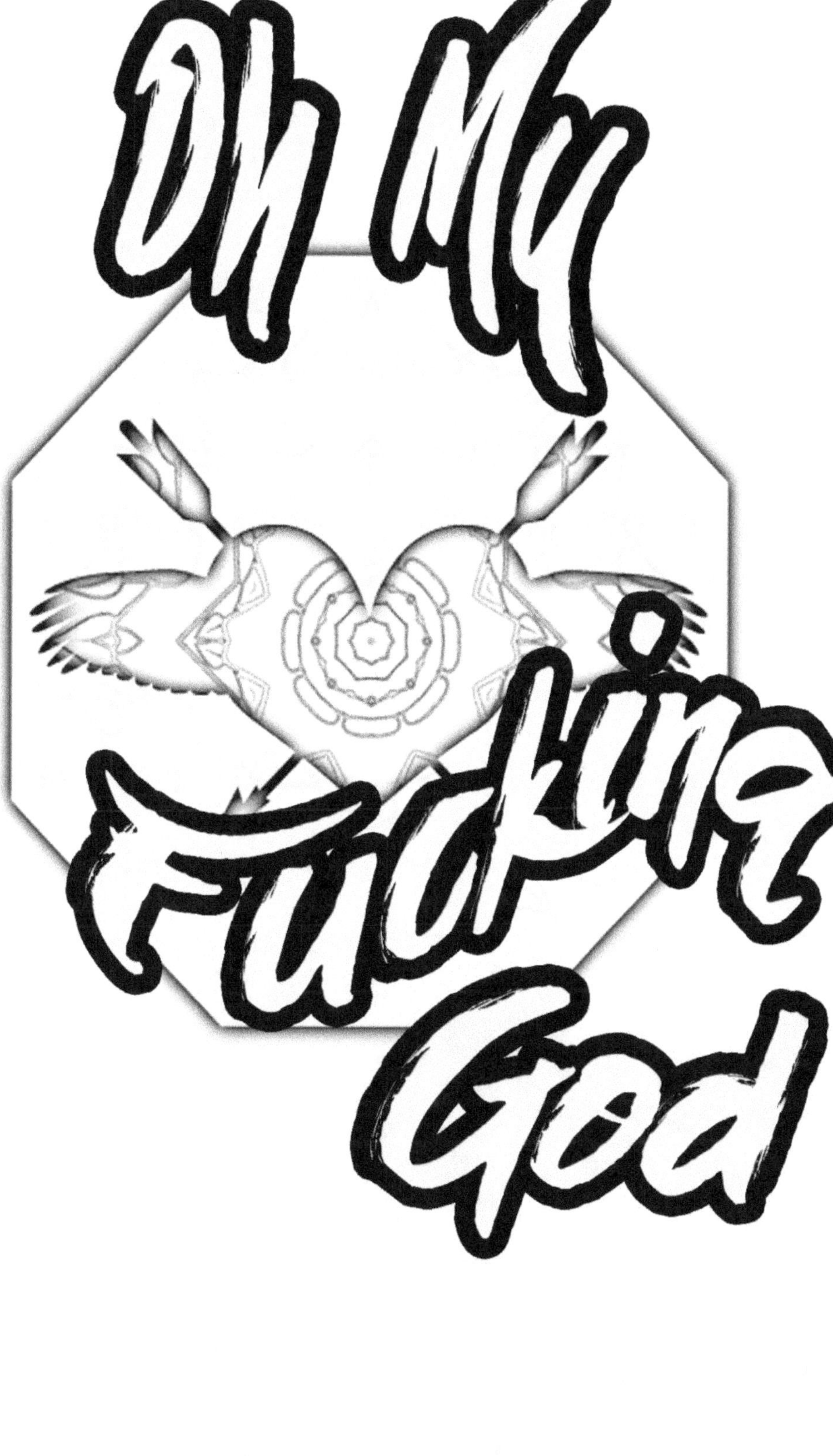
Oh My
Fucking
God

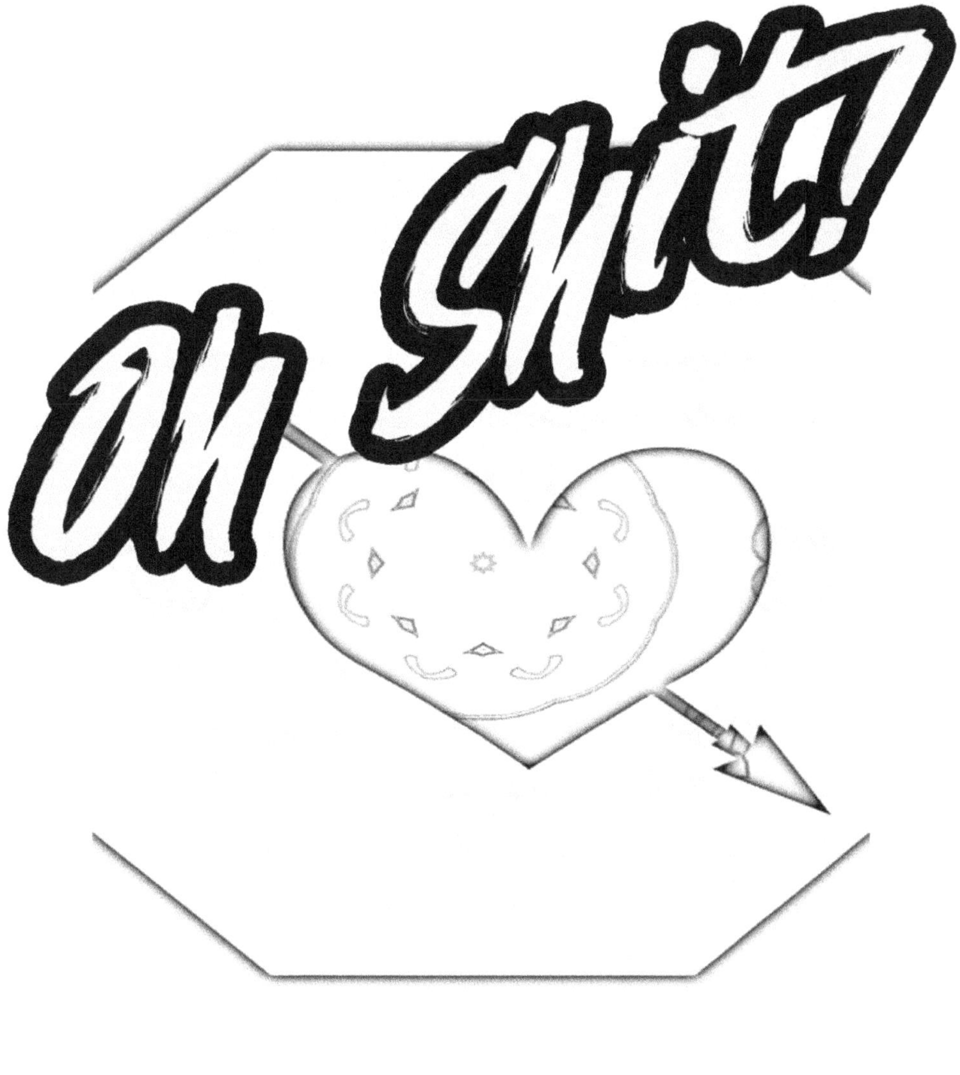
Oh Shit!

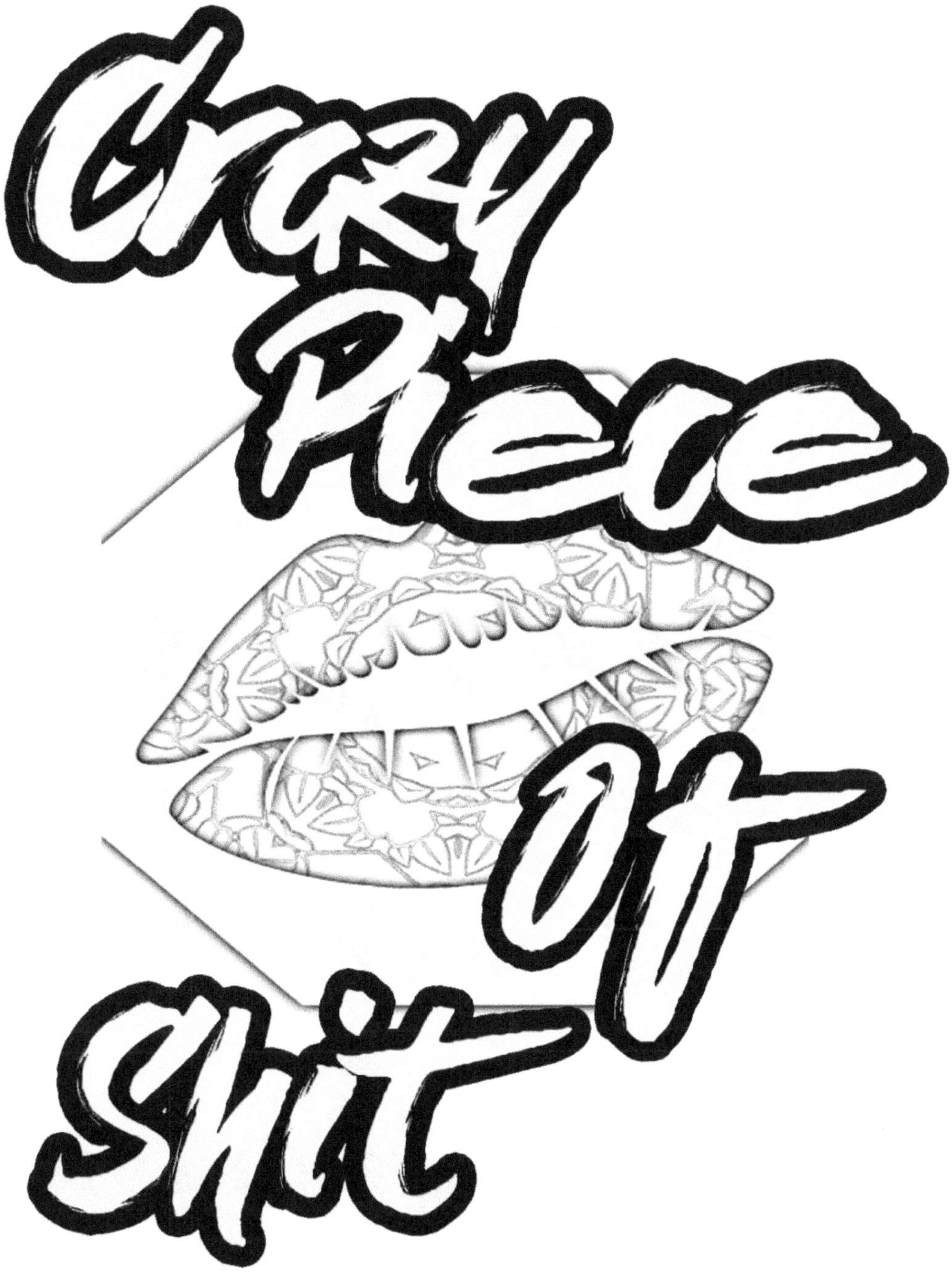
Crazy
Piece
Of
Shit

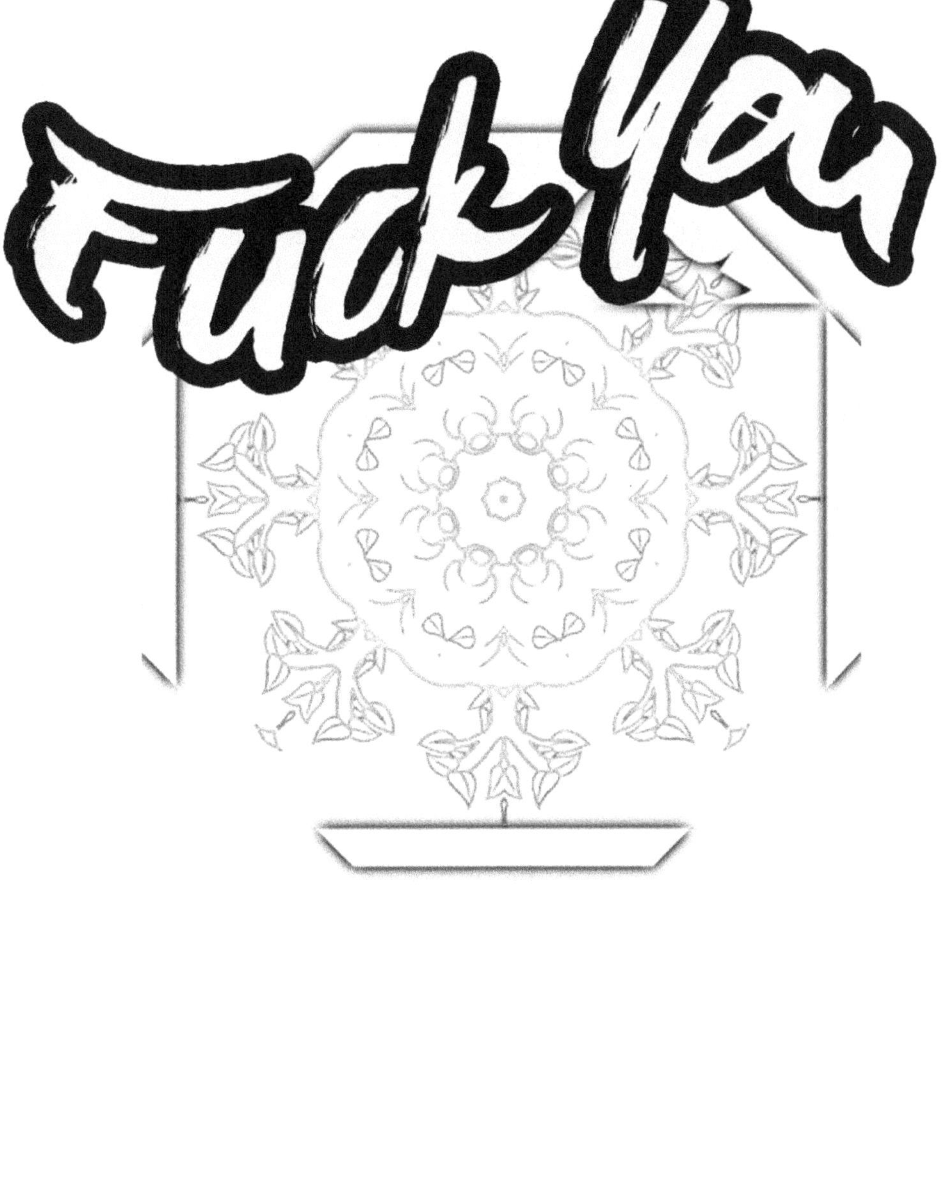
Fuck You

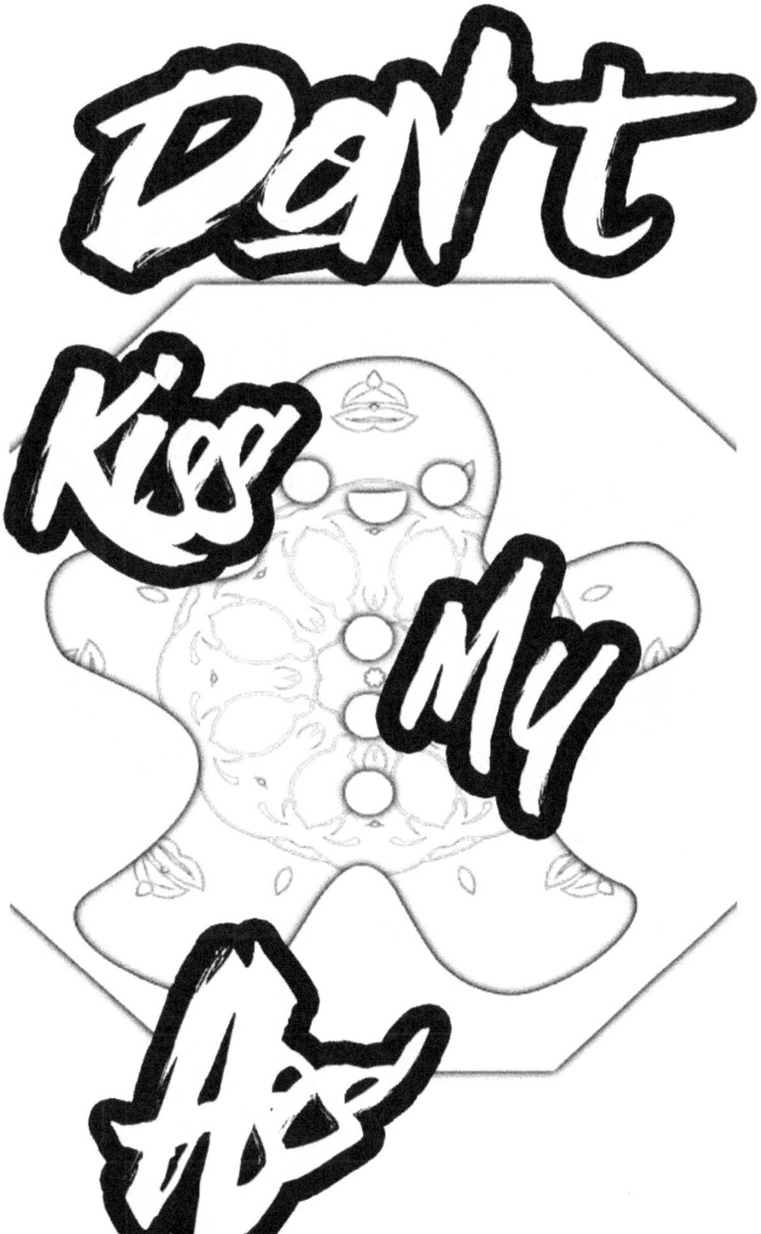
Don't
Kiss
My
Ass

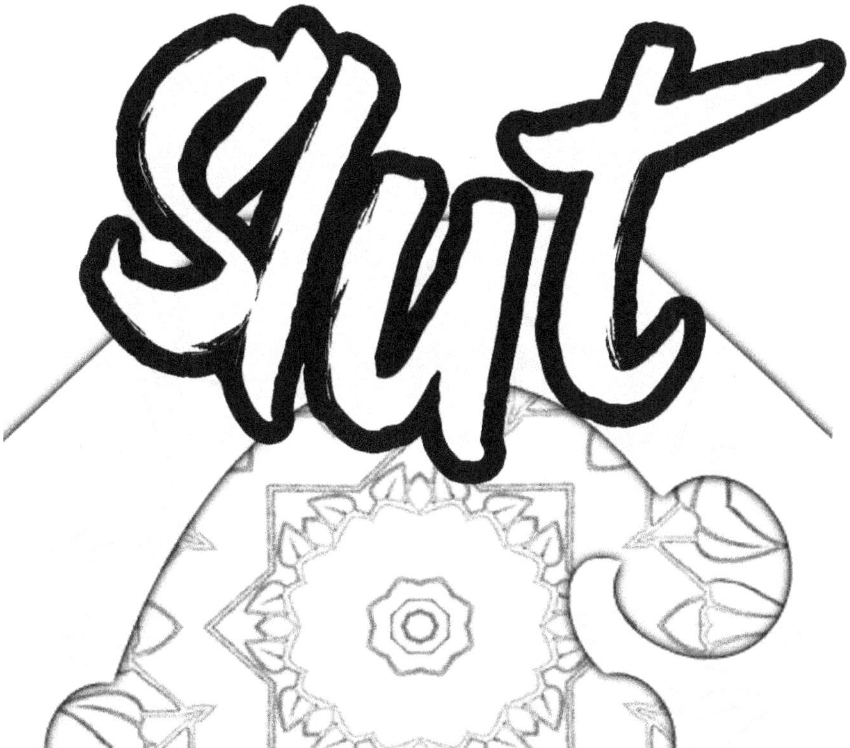
Slut

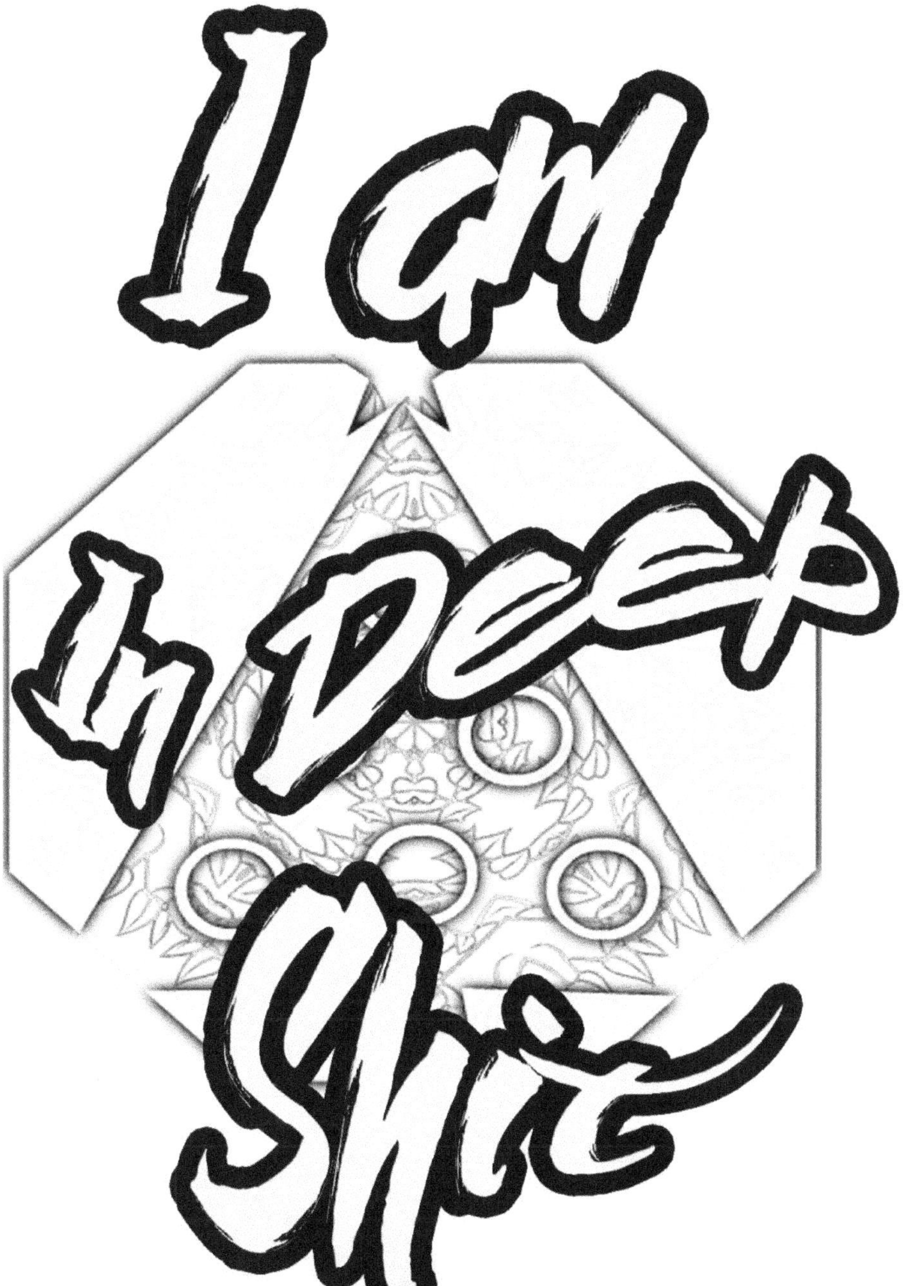
I am
In Deep
Shit

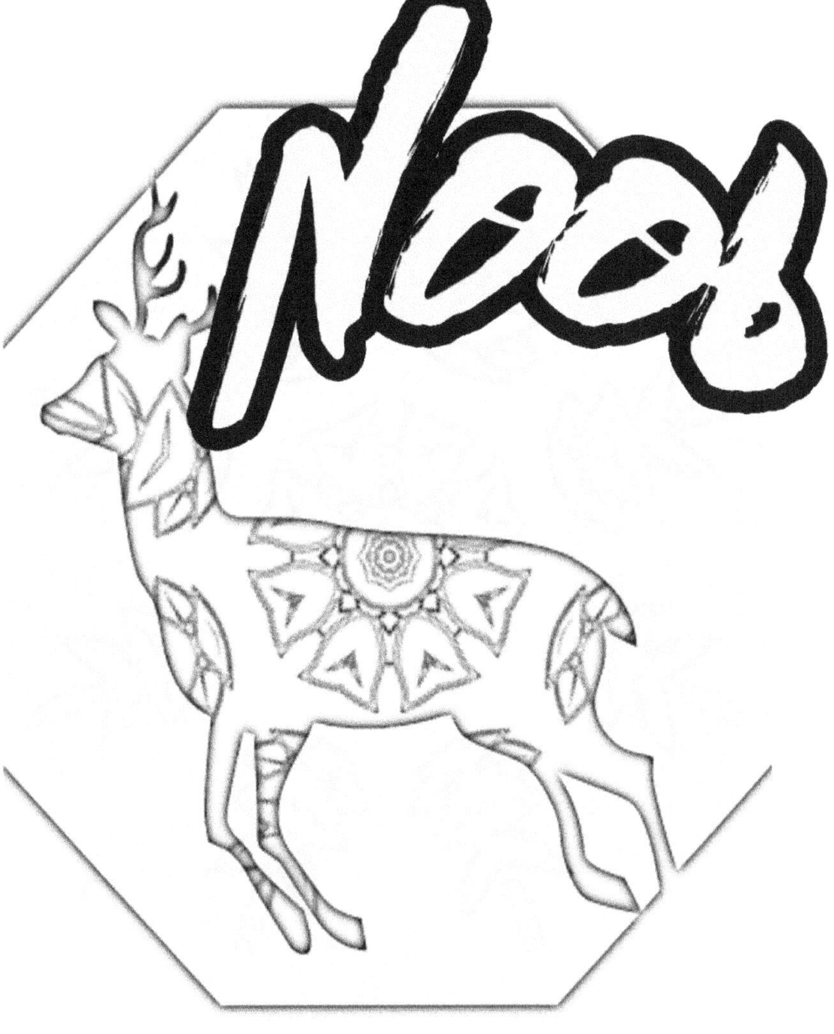
Noob

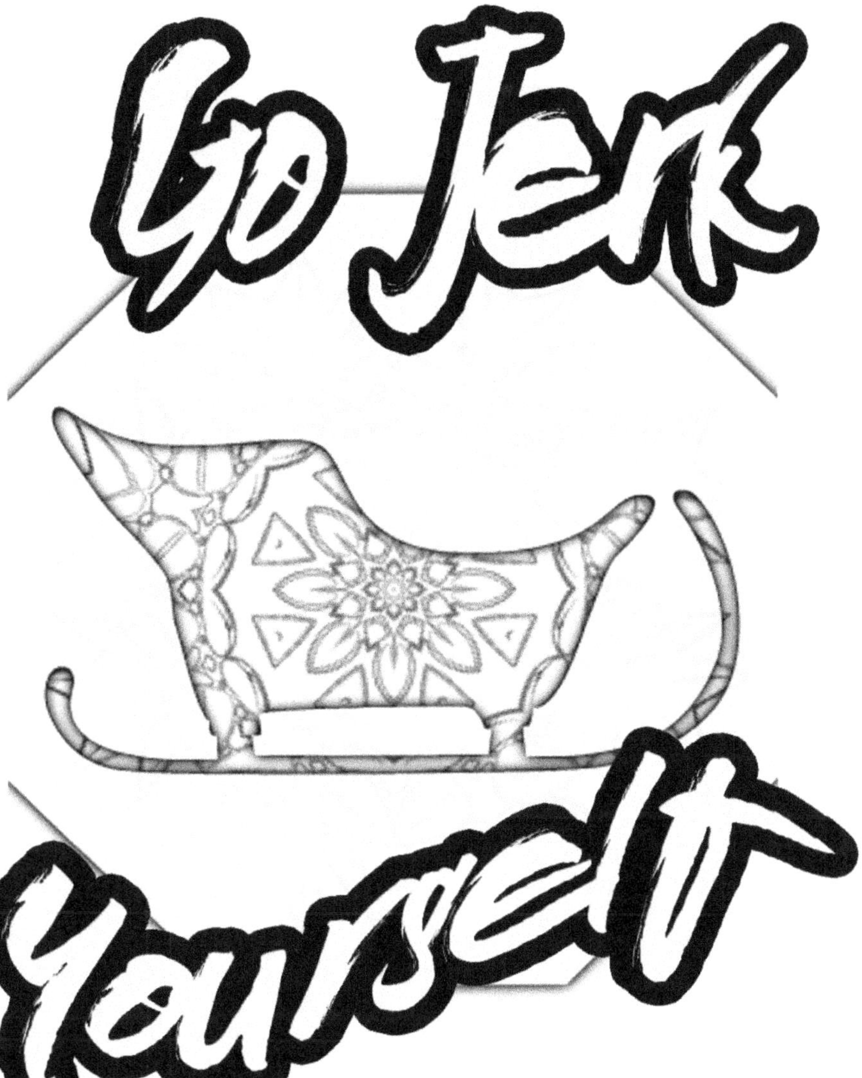
Go Jerk
Yourself

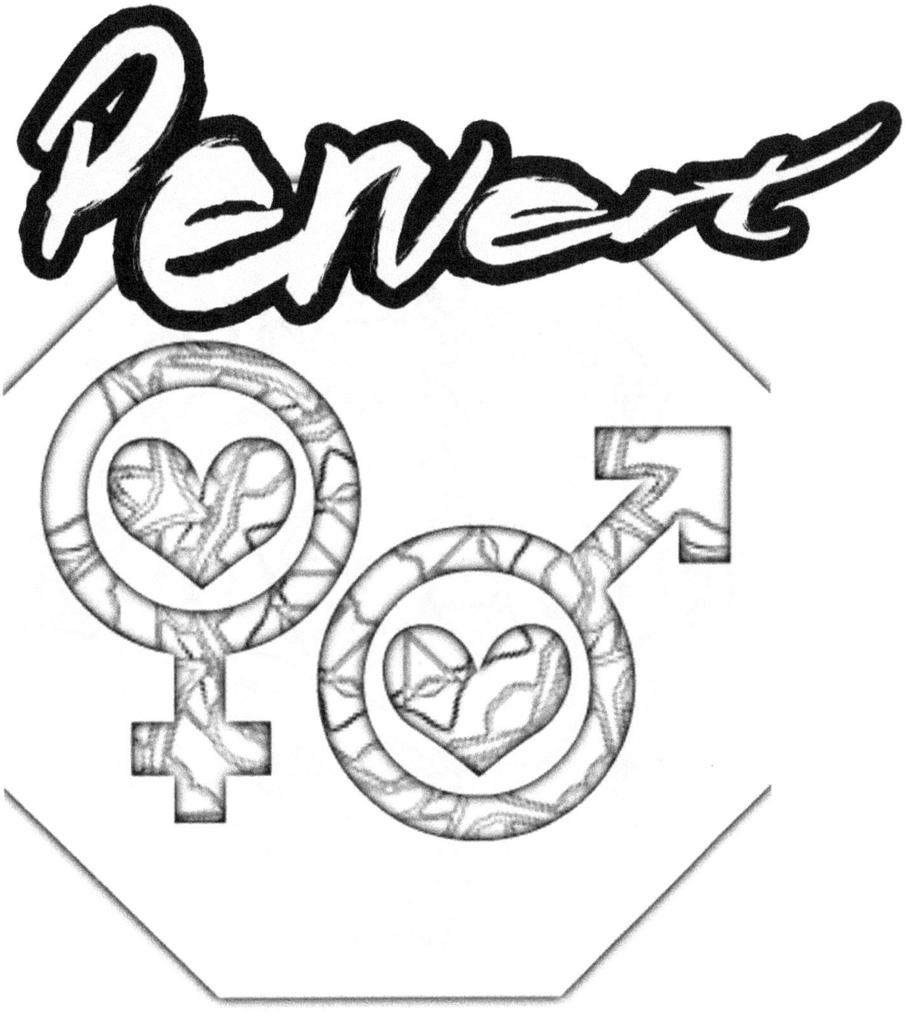
Pervert

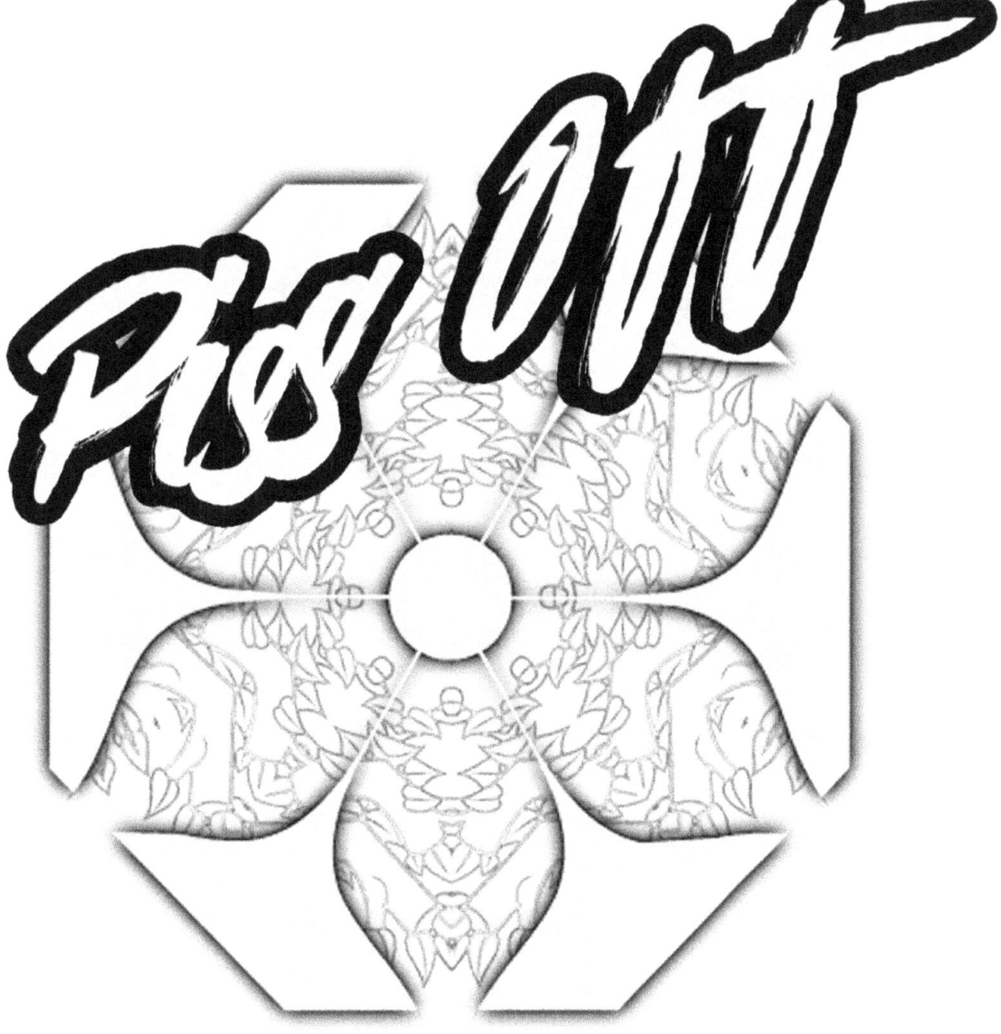
Piss Off

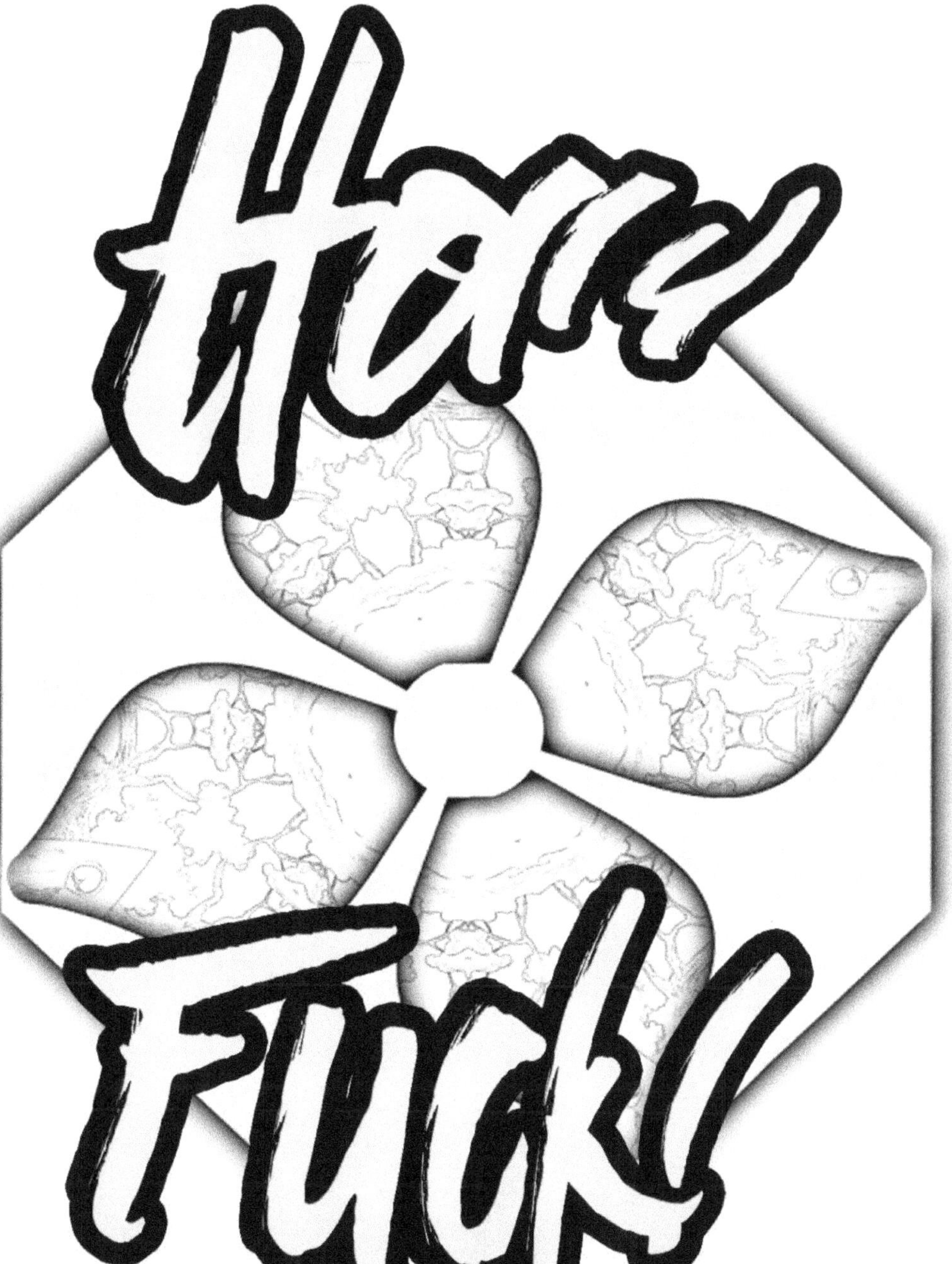
Hard
Fuck!

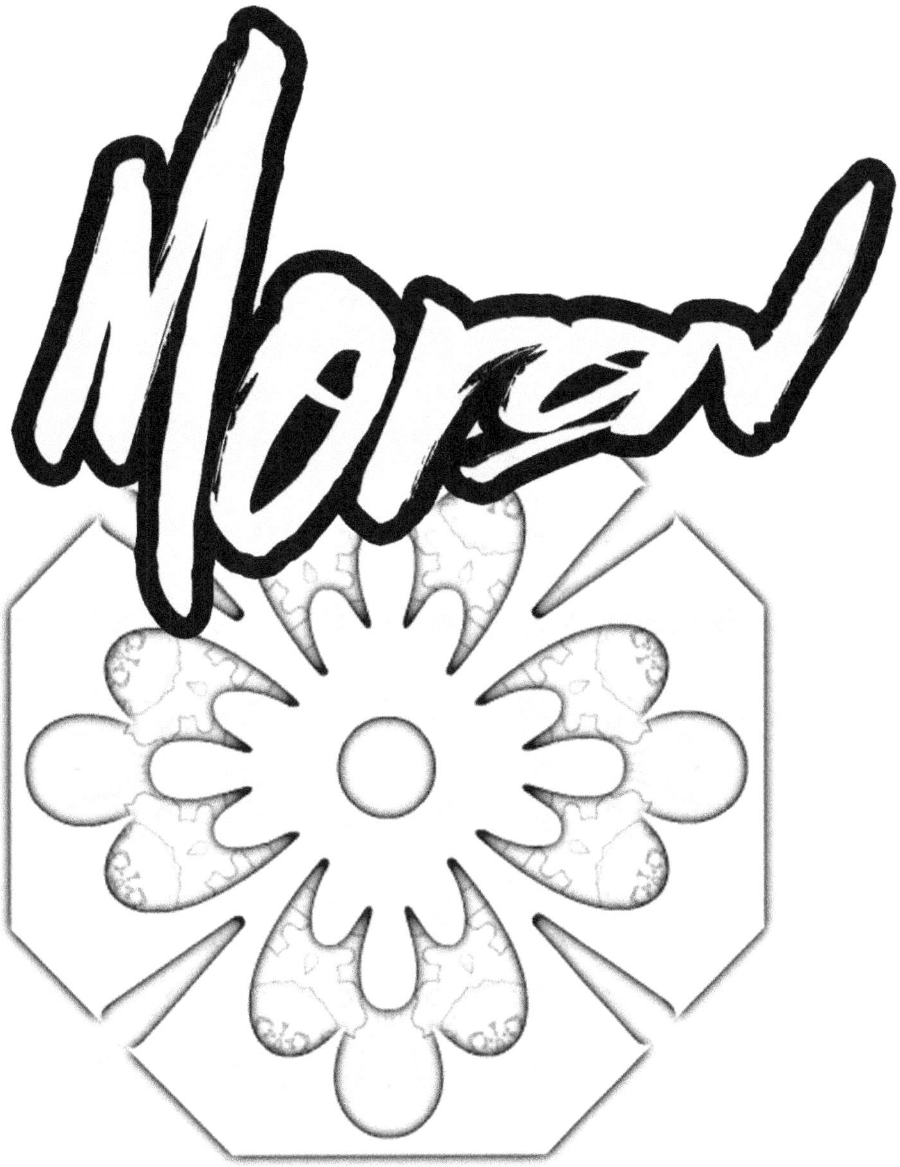

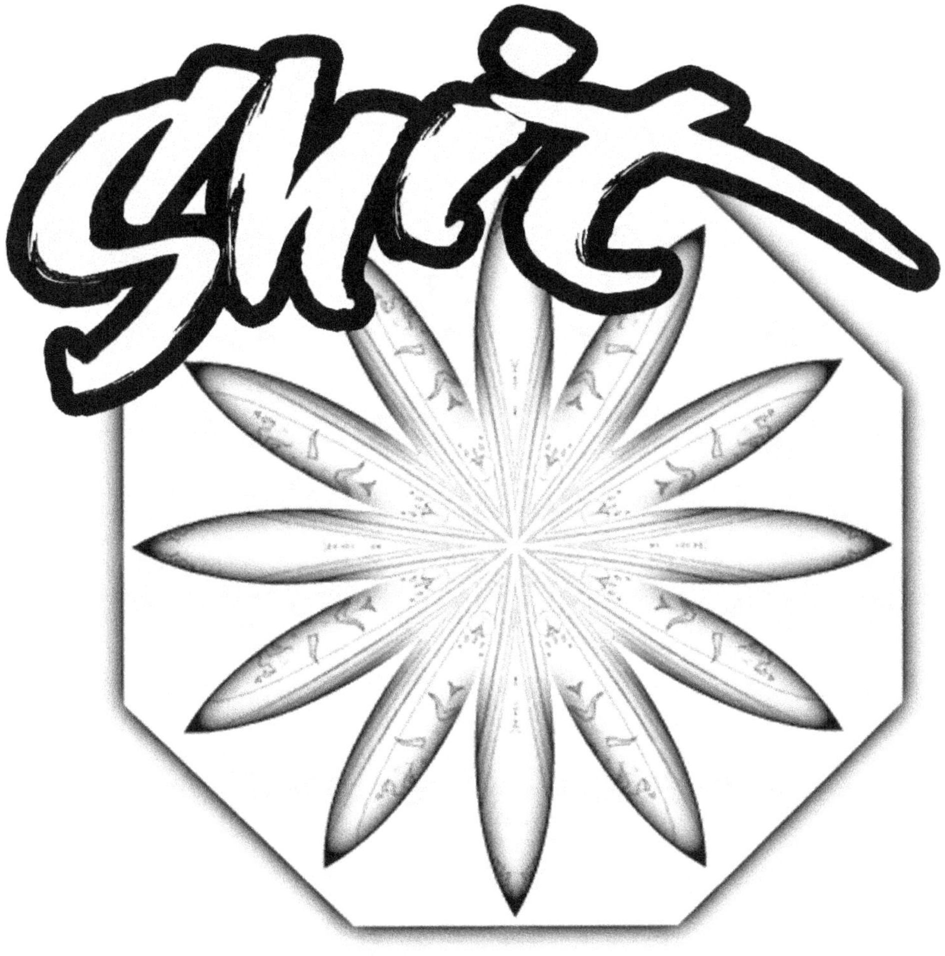
shit

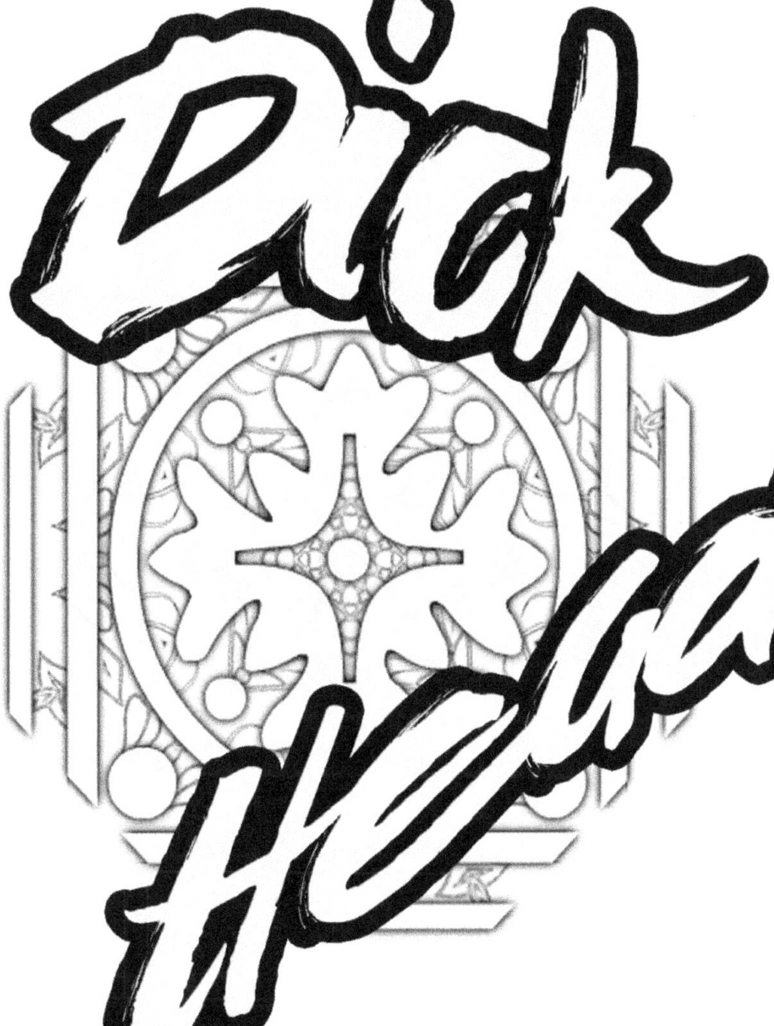
Dick
Head

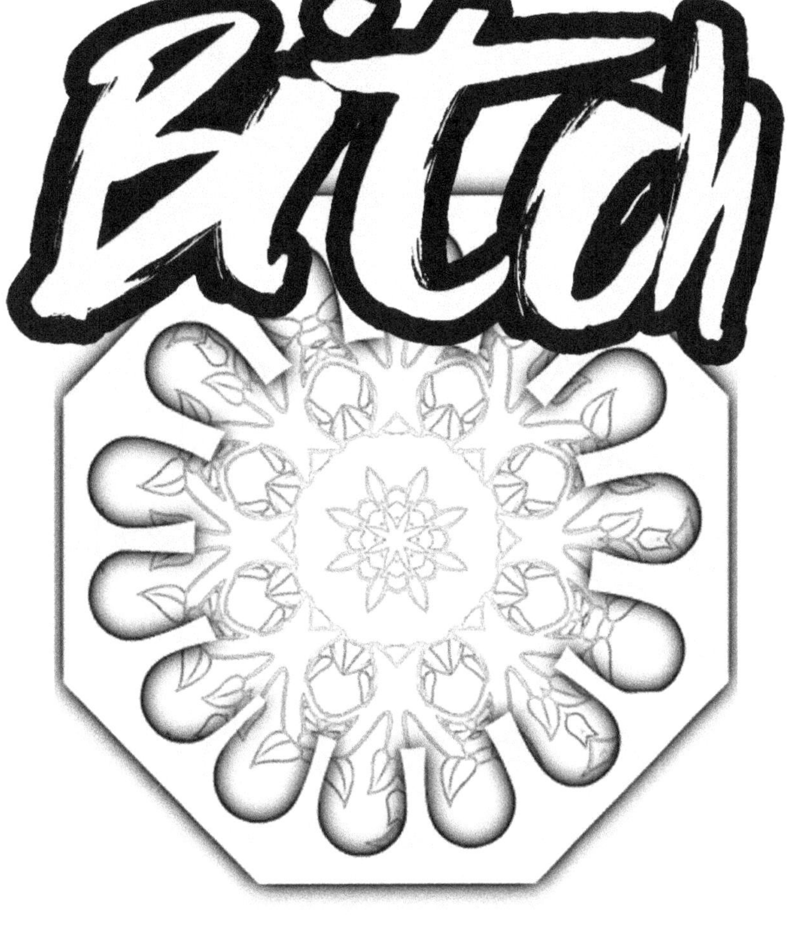
Bitch

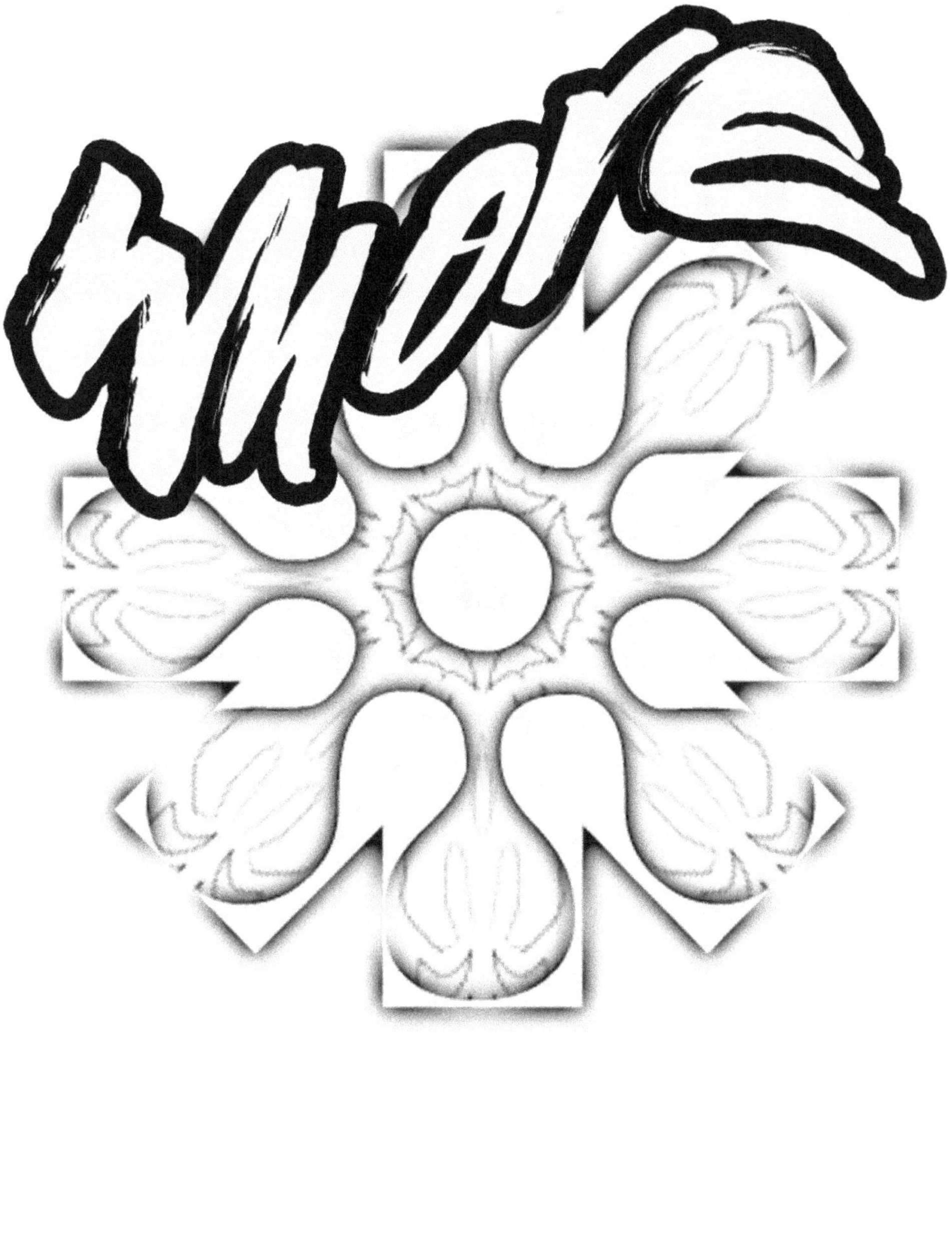
more

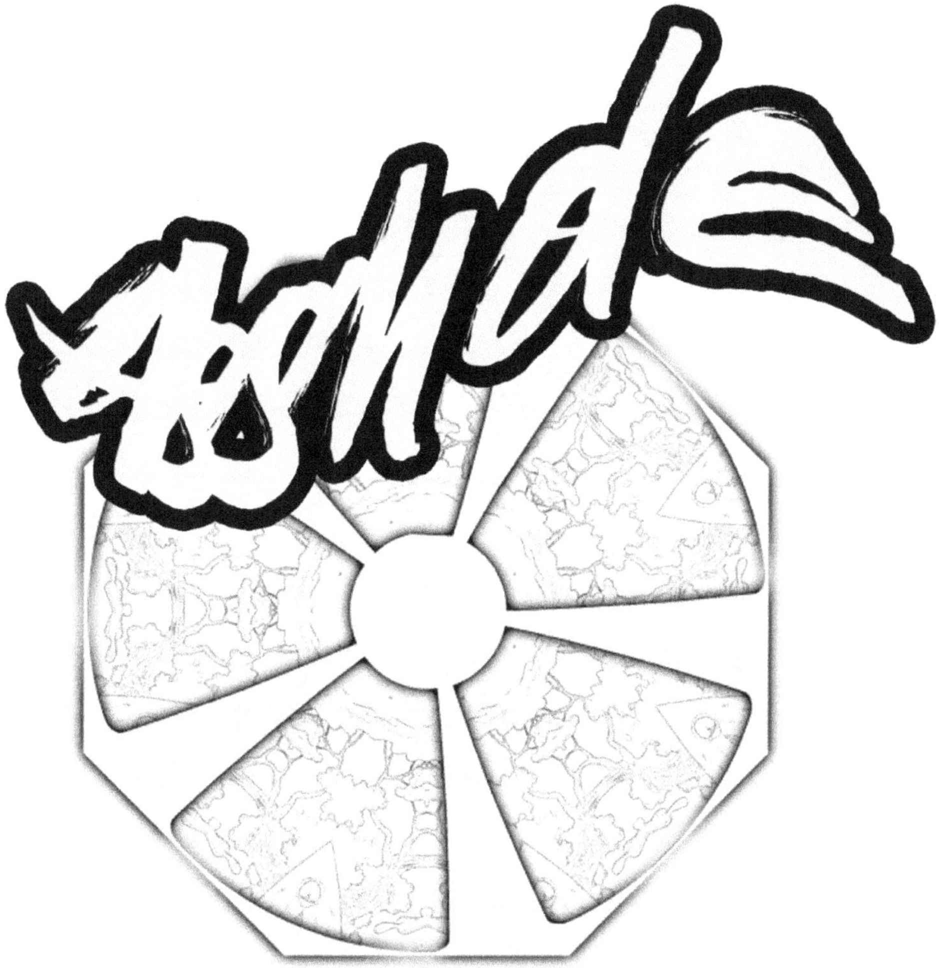

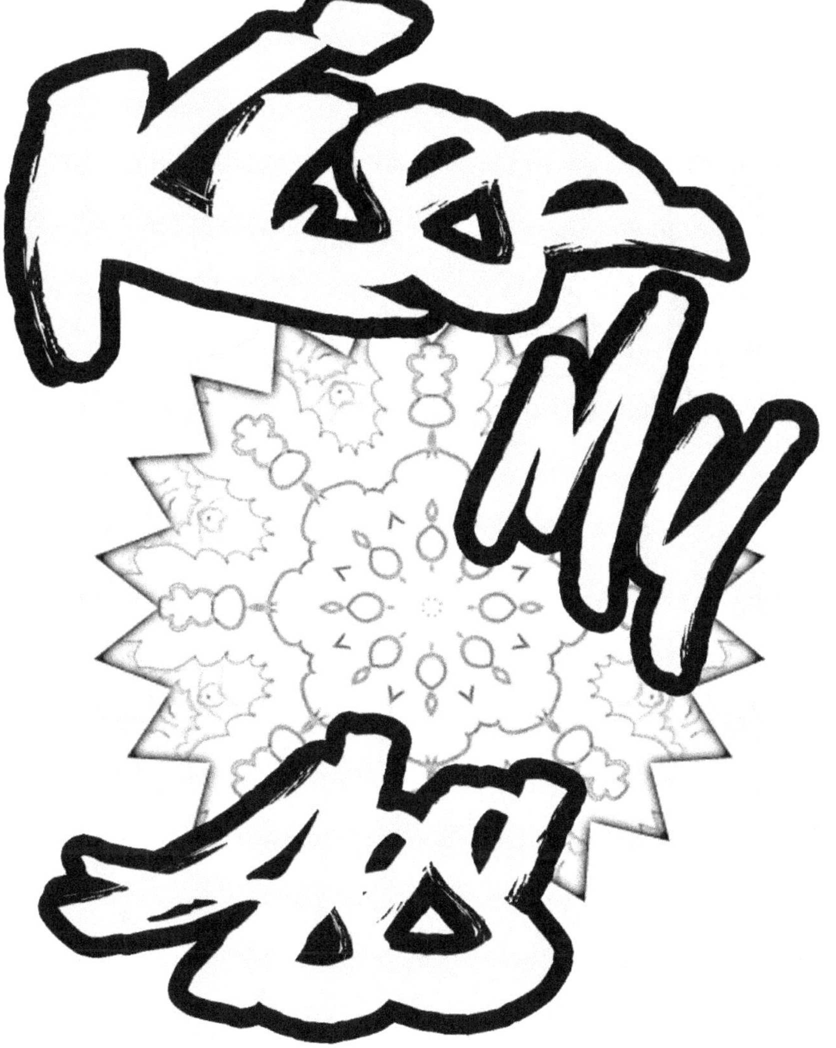
Kiss
My
Ass

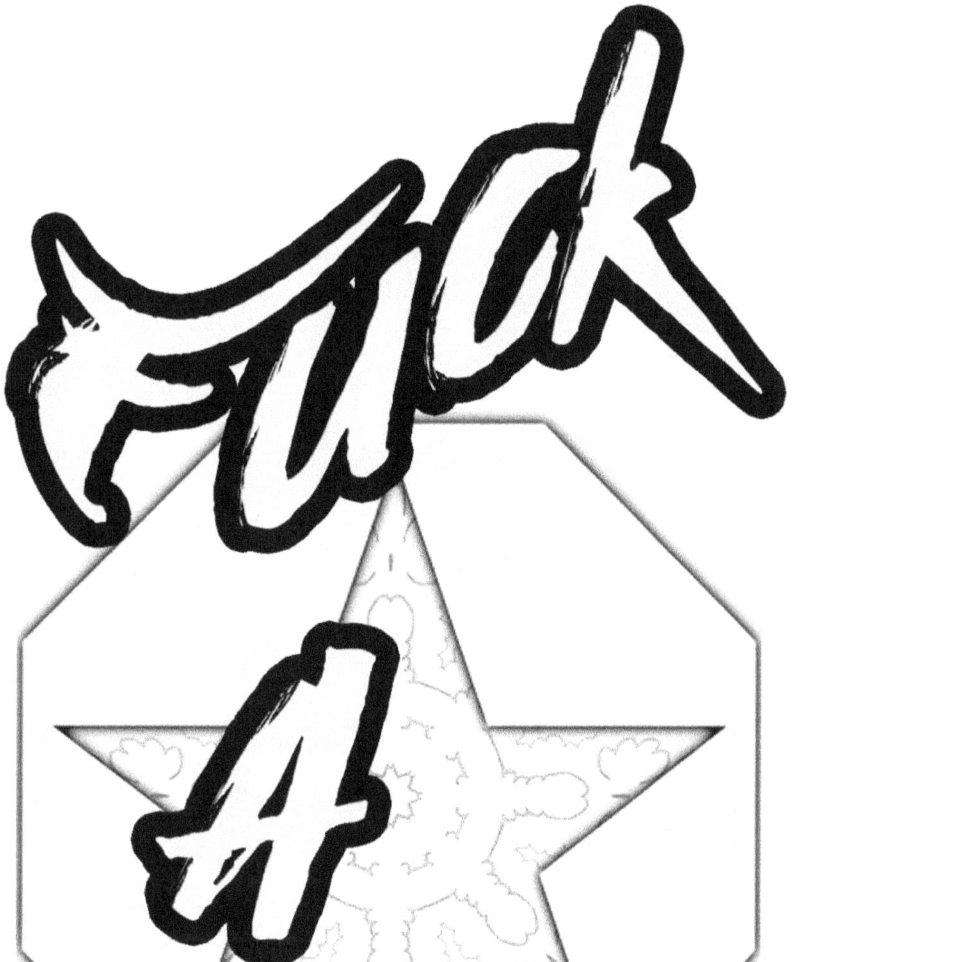
Fuck
A
Duck

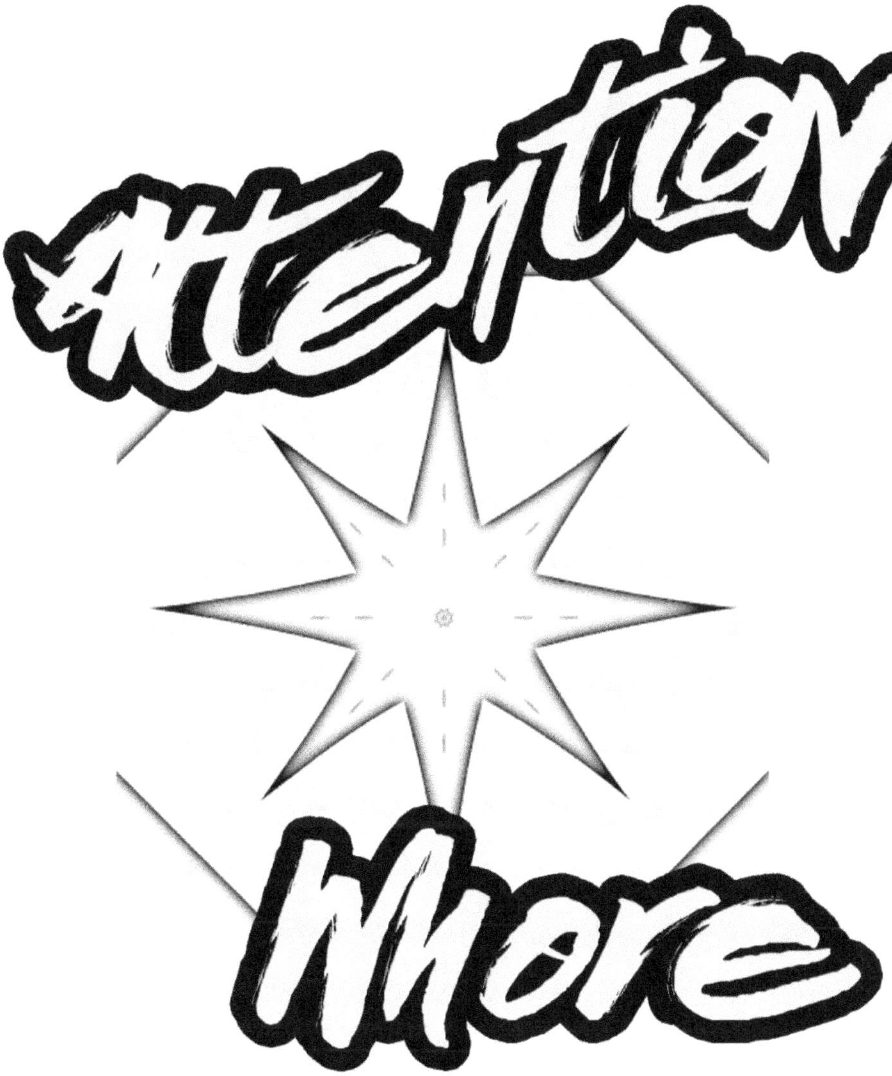

Attention
Whore

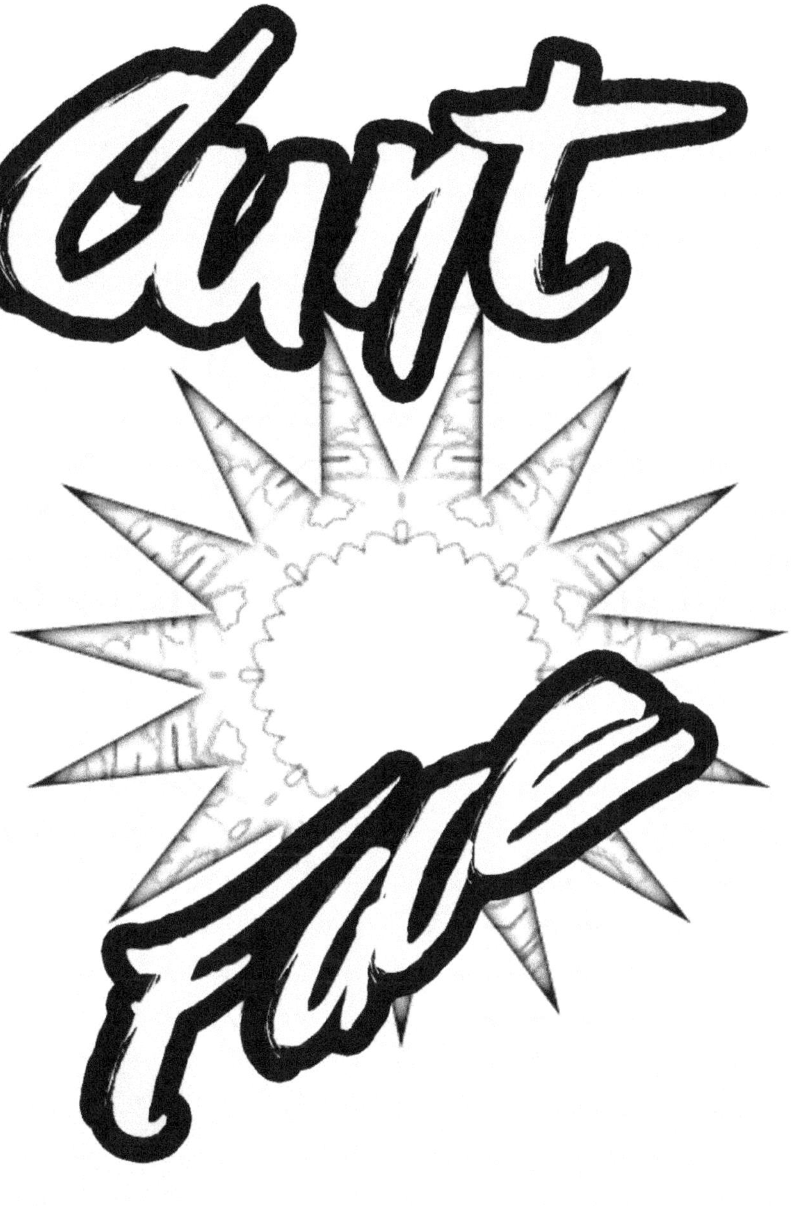
Cunt
Fail

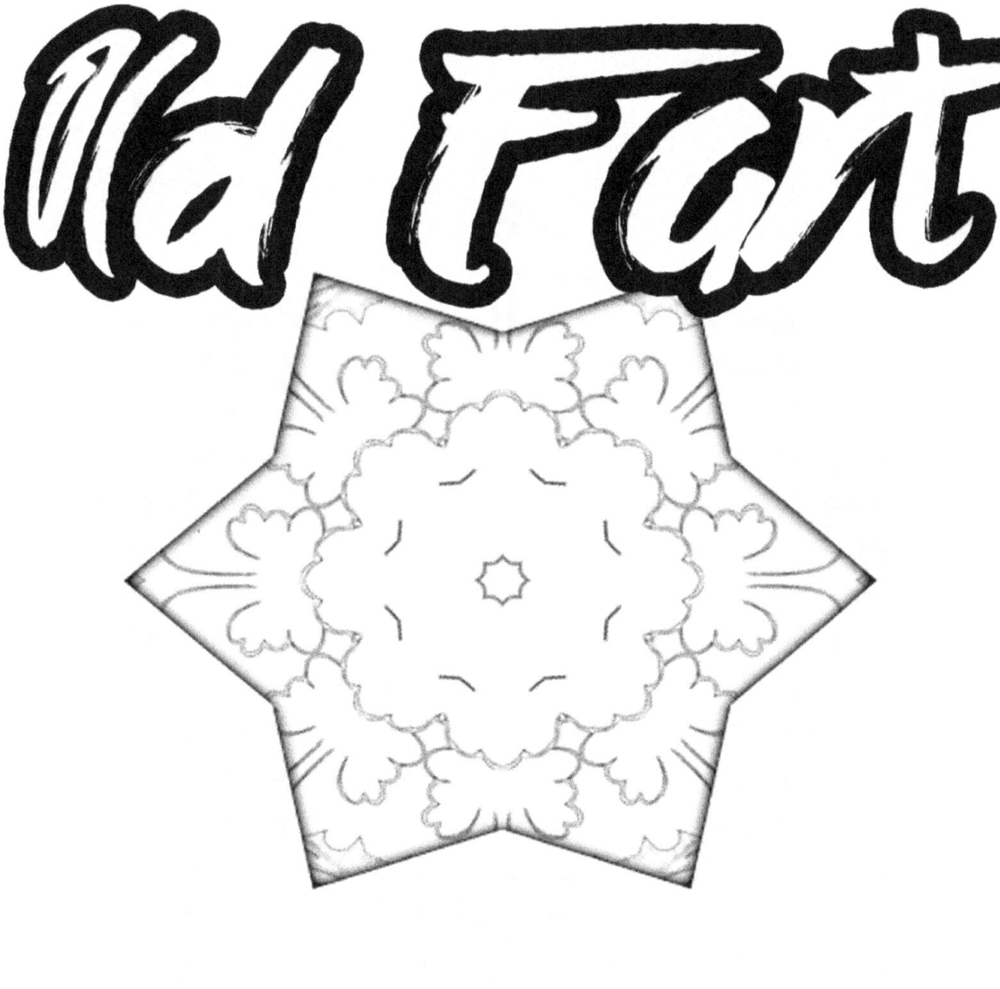
ld Fart

Note

www.ingramcontent.com/pod-product-compliance
Lightning Source LLC
Chambersburg PA
CBHW080637190526
45169CB00009B/3418
* 9 7 8 1 5 3 3 0 7 4 9 6 6 *